12 Annoying Monsters

self-talk for kids with **anxiety**

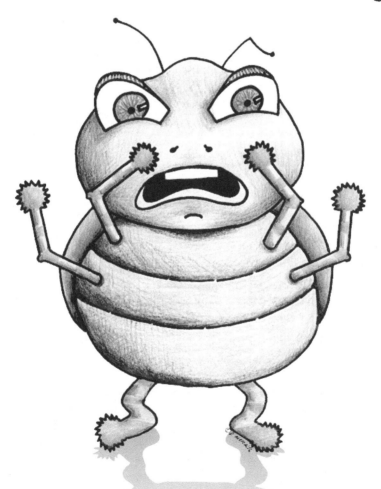

Written and Illustrated
by Dawn Meredith

I dedicate this book to you, the reader,

whoever and wherever you are.

There's a bond between us.

We know what it's like to be anxious.

This is an IndieMosh book
brought to you by MoshPit Publishing
an imprint of Mosher's Business Support Pty Ltd
PO Box 147
Hazelbrook NSW 2779

www.indiemosh.com.au

Copyright © Dawn Meredith 2014
Second edition

Author: 12 Annoying Monsters - Self-talk for kids with anxiety
Title: Meredith, Dawn
Illustrator: Meredith, Dawn

ISBNs: 978-0-9925046-8-7 (paperback)
               978-0-9925046-9-4 (epub)
               978-0-9925374-0-1 (mobi)

Contents

Foreword

When Dawn first advised me that she was writing a book about anxiety for young persons and was calling it '12 Annoying Monsters – Self Talk for Kids with Anxiety' I was immediately intrigued and excited! There is a much needed place for a book of this kind. I am sure there will be many parents and children clamoring to read it. I'll certainly be sending my own daughter a copy of it, and she is in her twenties!

I have had the pleasure of knowing Dawn for about eight years, and during that time I have never failed to be impressed by her exciting imagination, amazing creativity, and most of all, the deep compassion she has always shown for her students. It is the combination of these skills which has contributed to the success of her most recent endeavour.

In addition to her wide-reaching and gripping imaginative skills as a writer, Dawn has complemented this text by using her considerable artistic talent to illustrate each of the twelve annoying monsters who cause us all such anxiety. Her book is compelling. You just want to keep on reading. Most importantly, it is a book which we can all relate to, at some time in our lives, and this is the key to its success.

It takes skill to explain complex emotional issues in an accessible manner, whilst maintaining a rigorous pace, where the reader doesn't want to put the book down! Dawn has managed to achieve this difficult mix in her book.

Dawn gets straight into the nitty gritty. Her explanations about the brain, our senses, the role of adrenaline, and the way fears and anxieties play a part in all our lives, are informative, but also reassuring for young readers.

They offer a great deal of comfort to those children who may suffer from excessive anxiety at different times. And that is half the battle.

Reassurance is reinforced through understanding, so children are taught to identify the wide range of feelings which we all experience in our day to day lives. To assist with these understandings, Dawn has included some compelling, easy to complete exercises, which enhance a child's understandings and confidence.

This book is a gem because it not only explains the reasons for anxiety, it also offers practical and simple solutions for children in controlling it! Dawn explains that it is all about our thoughts, and that thoughts which might make us panic are like 'annoying monsters'. She also outlines the 'crooked thinking' which might lie behind the panic and how to overcome these wrong-footed beliefs. We can all relate to these monsters. I must confess that I particularly identify with the 'Bad Stuff Always Happens to Me' monster (in a constant state of perplexion), the 'It's all my Fault' monster, (who appears like a slug collapsed on the floor) and the 'Catastrophe' monster, (with the gaping mouth)!

I am sure Dawn's book will be a welcome addition to any parents' library and will be gobbled up by the children themselves!

Helen Hayward-Brown PhD, Dip. Teach

Hazelbrook March 2013

Thanks!

To all the friends, parents and students who have helped make this book possible. To Jamie Rees for help with layout and content, to Katie Vane and Anne Stanborough for feedback on the first major draft and to my husband, for his support, belief and enthusiasm for this book. And to Dr Helen Hayward-Brown for writing a wonderful foreword.

Why did I write this book?

A note from the author

I've worked with kids for many years; kids with all sorts of problems. And I've helped them. But I could not have written this book without them. Each one has taught me something valuable. So how do I know how it feels to be anxious? Well, I have a secret. I am an anxious person too! There have been times I've felt so anxious I thought I was going to vomit. And there have been times that I couldn't sleep. And times that I felt angry or cried for no reason. All these things can happen to someone who worries a lot. And I used to worry A LOT!

But I learned how to control it. My life is so much better! I still worry sometimes. It doesn't feel very nice, but I know I can make it go away because I have some helpful tricks to use.

There are lots and lots of kids who worry and feel quite sick about things at times. Something in their life might be changing and they worry about the new situation. They might try to do everything perfect to keep their parents happy. Some kids even have trouble sleeping because they worry so much. This can feel as if there's nothing they can do to change it. Perhaps this describes you.

So, are you ready to understand all about being anxious? Are you ready to find out how to control it? Read this book, discuss it with your parents/carers and learn about how your body and your mind try to protect you. Some of these 12 annoying monsters will make you giggle with their silly nonsense and you will see which ones talk to you and what you can do to ignore them. I hope you enjoy my book and find some useful bits of information to help you worry less.
It's going to be great! See you at the end of the book.
Best wishes, Dawn x
PS I've left the monsters as just black and white drawings so that you can colour them in, if you wish.

Chapter One

What's Happening to Me?

Introduction

So, you're a bit anxious sometimes. Or perhaps a lot. That's OK! You are not alone. Lots and lots of people feel anxious at times. Read on! This book will explain:

- what anxiety actually is
- why it's a natural thing your body does to protect you
- how you can learn to switch it off when it gets overpowering

Wouldn't that be awesome?

You don't have to be afraid of anxiety. You can control it. Let's begin with what happens inside your body. It all starts in your brain...

Your brain is boss!

Your brain and your body are partners. They are connected. Your brain is like an instructor. It tells your body to do things, such as run, sit down, pick up something or scratch your nose.

There are also *automatic* things your brain tells your body to do. It tells your heart to keep beating and pumping. It tells your lungs to keep filling with air and then pushing it out. It tells your stomach to digest the food you eat. It even tells you to yawn! You don't have to think about these things because your brain organizes it for you. They are automatic.

Now here's something super cool! It also works in reverse. Your body tells your brain what's happening to it. It's called 'feedback'. It tells your brain when you're sleepy, tired, hungry or hurt.

The Five Senses

Your brain also gets feedback from your five senses:
- your ears, (everything you hear)
- your eyes, (everything you see)
- your skin, (everything you touch & what touches you)
- your nose, (everything you smell)
- your tongue, (everything you taste)

All these things are processed in your brain without you having to think about it.

It looks a bit like broccoli, doesn't it? This is your brain as viewed from the side.

But there's another part of your brain: *your mind.*

It is here that you have another sense. Your sense of *feeling* or *knowing.* Inside your mind is where thoughts are made. Your mind is constantly thinking, analyzing, questioning, even if you are not aware of it. Thoughts pop into your mind all the time and your brain hears them all. And here's the most important thing -

It *believes* whatever you think.

Sometimes your thoughts become feelings, like when you're happy, or sad or curious or angry or something is funny. Your brain is listening to those feelings and sometimes sends signals down into your body. If something is funny, you laugh.

If something is sad, you cry. When you're scared, your body gets ready to do something amazing.

Fight or Flight

When you're frightened, your brain tells your heart to start pumping faster, to get more blood to your legs in case you need to run away from danger. Your brain also pumps more blood to your arms, in case you have to fight your way out.

This is called 'Fight or Flight". It can cause tingling in your arms and legs and it might feel like there's a horse galloping inside your chest. You might also feel hot and sweaty.

This is perfectly normal. Your brain is keeping you safe by alerting you to danger and preparing your body to be ready either to fight or run away. After a while, when you feel safe again, your brain calms things down and everything returns to normal.

Adrenaline

Fight or flight is a reaction to your thoughts. This means, if you see something that might be dangerous, a thought pops into your mind like:

"I don't like this! I could get hurt!"

Your brain believes what your mind thinks and so it swings into action to keep you safe. Suddenly you *feel* scared. Your heart is pumping wildly and your legs and arms are tingly. This is because your brain sends a signal to all those parts of the body using a chemical called adrenaline. Adrenaline rushes around inside your body extremely fast, telling it to get ready to fight or run. Sometimes adrenaline will give you a tight feeling in your chest. In this amazing way, your body looks after you. Your brain directs things. And your thoughts make your mind very, very powerful.

Anxiety

But what if you were scared for no reason? What if you weren't actually in any danger? What if you just *thought* something bad was going to happen? Your brain believes your mind's thoughts, remember. It would tell your body to get ready to run, even though there is nothing to run from.

One little thought can control everything. When little things cause a super big reaction of fear we call the thoughts 'anxiety' or 'being anxious'.

Anxiety starts in your mind with a single thought. It could be you're about to have a spelling test and you're worried you won't know the words, or a Maths test and you're worried you can't remember how to do the sums.

The thought that pops into your mind might be something like this:

"Oh no! I'm going to fail this spelling test!"

"I *always* do badly at Maths!"

"I'm a hopeless speller! I never get them right!"

Once that thought pops into your mind, your brain believes there is real danger and adrenaline starts to rush around your body. You feel hot and sweaty. Your hands are shaky. Your mouth goes dry. You're breathing too hard and there's a tight feeling in your chest or stomach. You start to 'panic'. Fear of failing the test has made your body think there is real danger. But there isn't.

'Normal' Fears

So, is there such a thing? Yes. Of course. It's normal to have fears. Fears keep us safe. And they change as we grow older and understand the world around us more. When we are little, we might be afraid of the dark, or getting separated from Mum, or storms. In Primary School we might not feel afraid of those things anymore and develop new fears, such as meeting new people, being in new situations, spiders, being bullied, injections, burglary in our home and being laughed at. We might also be concerned someone we love will get hurt. These are 'normal' fears that lots of kids have. By the time we get to high school only a couple of those fears remain, such as being laughed at, meeting new people, or bad things happening to us on the bus etc.

We now understand that even if we don't particularly *like* spiders, we can avoid them. We know that storms are a natural part of the weather and don't hurt us, even though they are loud. We no longer fear Mum and Dad leaving us because we actually want them to leave us alone sometimes! Getting older means learning what is real and what isn't. We like to be proud of ourselves, to be able to do things ourselves, without help.

So, when do normal fears become 'abnormal'? The simple answer is - when they start to take over. *When they stop us doing the things we love.*

What are you afraid of?

Here's a little exercise to help you identify what it is that you fear or are anxious about: Say this and fill in the missing bit –

"I am scared of _____ because _____"

"When I'm scared it stops me from _____"

"If I wasn't scared, I would be able to _____"

How Fears Affect Your Body

We've talked about how your body protects you, how it prepares you for fight or flight. Let's see if you can identify the feelings in your body you get when you are scared about something.

FEAR OF	What my body feels

Chapter Two

The Names of Feelings

When we're little, we have a small vocabulary. That is, we only know a few words. As babies all we can do is cry to communicate with our parents. If our nappy is wet and uncomfortable we can't say, "Excuse me, but my nappy needs changing. It's really uncomfortable." All we can do is cry and if they don't listen, cry louder! Mothers are very good at figuring out what is wrong just by the different ways a baby cries. A cry for hunger is different to a cry because the baby is tired and needs a sleep. Some experts think a mother knows up to seven different cries!

As we grow and learn to speak we get better at communicating. Not only can we tell people what we're feeling, but we can ask questions about things we want to know. We learn new words every day which all goes into our memory bank and becomes part of our language.

So, feeling words. There are lots of them. Instead of just saying "I feel bad," we can be a lot more specific. We can say, "I feel irritated," or "I feel frightened." It's very useful for others to know exactly what we are feeling so they can help us.

Here's some scales to show different emotions, from relaxed all the way up to stronger emotions and some of the mood steps in between.

RAGE

— Furious

— Angry

— Annoyed

— Irritated

— Frustrated

— Disappointed

Relaxed

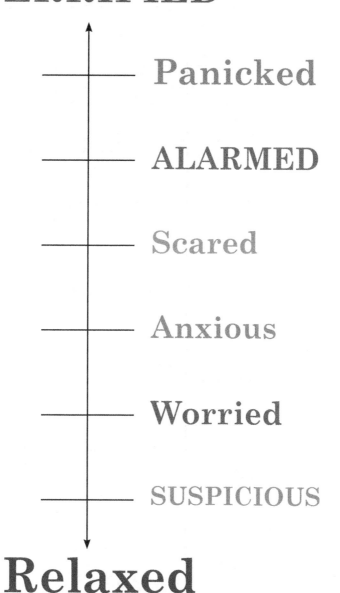

TERRIFIED

Panicked

ALARMED

Scared

Anxious

Worried

SUSPICIOUS

Relaxed

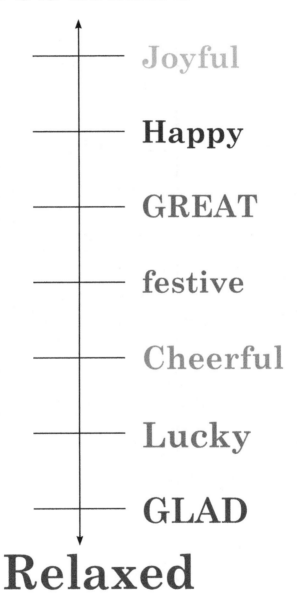

ECSTATIC

Joyful

Happy

GREAT

festive

Cheerful

Lucky

GLAD

Relaxed

Here are some lists of emotions to help you identify how you might be feeling sometimes. Use it whenever you want to explain to someone how you're feeling but you're not sure which word to use. If you need it, use a dictionary to help you with meanings.

Pleasant Feelings

OPEN	HAPPY	ALIVE	GOOD
understanding	great	playful	calm
confident	merry	courageous	peaceful
reliable	joyous	energetic	reassured
easy	lucky	liberated	comfortable
amazed	fortunate	optimistic	pleased
free	delighted	provocative	encouraged
sympathetic	overjoyed	impulsive	clever
interested	cheerful	free	surprised
satisfied	thankful	frisky	content
receptive	important	wonderful	quiet
accepting	festive	spirited	certain
kind	ecstatic	thrilled	relaxed
	satisfied		serene
	glad		free and easy

LOVE	INTERESTED	POSITIVE	STRONG
loving	concerned	eager	impulsive
considerate	affected	keen	free
affectionate	fascinated	earnest	sure
sensitive	intrigued	intent	certain
tender	absorbed	anxious	rebellious
devoted	inquisitive	inspired	unique
attracted	nosy	determined	dynamic
passionate	snoopy	excited	tenacious
admiration	engrossed	enthusiastic	hardy
warm	curious	hopeful	secure
touched		challenged	bold
sympathy		optimistic	brave
close		confident	daring
loved			
comforted			

Difficult/Unpleasant Feelings

ANGRY	DEPRESSED	CONFUSED	HELPLESS
irritated	lousy	upset	useless
enraged	disappointed	doubtful	alone
hostile	discouraged	uncertain	paralyzed
insulting	ashamed	indecisive	tired
sore	powerless	perplexed	dominated
annoyed	miserable	embarrassed	inferior
upset	guilty	hesitant	vulnerable
cross	dissatisfied	shy	empty
unpleasant	a sense of loss	distrustful	forced
boiling	detestable	unsure	hesitant
bitter	terrible	uneasy	despair
aggressive	despicable	skeptical	frustrated
resentful	in despair	tense	distressed
indignant	sulky	pessimistic	woeful
infuriated	dejected	lost	pathetic
fuming			tragic

INDIFFERENT	AFRAID	HURT	SAD
insensitive	fearful	crushed	tearful
dull	terrified	tormented	sorrowful
nonchalant	suspicious	deprived	pained
neutral	anxious	wronged	grief
reserved	alarmed	tortured	anguish
weary	panicked	alienated	desolate
bored	nervous	rejected	desperate
preoccupied	scared	injured	pessimistic
cold	worried	offended	unhappy
disinterested	frightened	humiliated	lonely
lifeless	timid	aching	dismayed
	shaky	victimized	
	restless	heartbroken	
	doubtful	agonized	
	threatened	appalled	
	cowardly		
	wary		

Feelings and understanding others

Feelings aren't just emotions *you* have. Everyone has them! And in order to be happy, we need to understand and recognize the feelings of our family and friends. That way we know how to react to them. If your sister is feeling sad, you don't go and jump all over her or yell "TAG!" and run off. If your dad is telling you off for something naughty you did, it is not appropriate to laugh. Just as your expressions give others clues to your own feelings, you need also to learn how to notice the expressions and body language of others. It's a skill.

Most people have no problem learning to read these facial and body 'cues'. As they grow, they learn and become more accurate and *sensitive*. But some people have difficulty recognizing how others feel. They might interpret the expression they see inaccurately. For example, if your friend looks really happy and you think they are mad at you and you react with, "What's the matter with you? I haven't done anything!" This could make life pretty confusing! Seeing as we all want to get along with people and feel accepted, it's a good idea to check that our skills in recognizing the emotions of others is on target.

Match these signs of face & body language to their meanings:

Folded arms	sad, unhappy
Frowning	really happy, not just being polite
Raised eyebrows	unimpressed, annoyed, irritated
Waving, smiling	angry, don't want to listen
Looking down, bottom lip sticking out	asking a question, mild surprise
Tight mouth, squinted eyes, looking away	concentrating, thinking
Smile with crinkling around the eyes	happy to see you

Now draw a line to match these face expressions to the feeling words:

joyful

sad

annoyed

angry

disdainful

scared

worried

pleased

surprised

Chapter Three

What Can I do?

Mindfulness

Let's go back to 'fight or flight' for a moment. Truthfully, it is not a nice feeling. It's like your whole world is exploding, like everything is happening all at once and you have no control over it. Your body tingles, your heart is beating like crazy, you're sweaty and your mouth is dry.

But hey, guess what? You DO have some control over those uncomfortable, over-the-top reactions of fear, when there's actually no danger.

So, how do you control it?

Remember how everything starts in the mind, with one little thought? That's where you control it, before your brain starts directing an escape plan for your body. The first step to being able to control that unhelpful thought is being aware that you're thinking it. This is called *mindfulness*.

Your inner recording

All of us have a collection of familiar thoughts which replay in our head all the time. They come from many years of thinking the same way. Some of these thoughts are things other people have said that we've stored in there. Sometimes they're great! Like this one –

I'm really proud of you!

Unfortunately, they can sometimes be not-so-nice, unhelpful thoughts, whizzing around inside your head.

For example:

> You're hopeless!
>
> I'm so disappointed in you right now!
>
> Ha, ha! You got it wrong!

And sometimes they are thoughts we have created from feelings we've had –

> I've never been any good at sport and I never will be.
>
> or
>
> It's a waste of time trying, because I never get it right.

Just like a CD, these recordings can repeat over and over. They have the power to make you feel pretty sad or upset. <u>Unless you stop the track from playing</u>.

Being mindful means that you recognise them at once as those recordings. Once you recognise what's playing, you can *switch* tracks to something more helpful.

Unhelpful thought -

> "Ah! A spelling test! I always fail at these!

Helpful thought -

> I'm just going to do the best I can. And that's alright.

With this more helpful kind of thought you are doing 3 important things:

1. Being honest with yourself – you're not very confident about getting all the words right. But hey, no one is perfect.

2. Telling yourself that you're going to be brave and try anyway. Good one!

3. Realising that even if you don't get them all correct, it's still ok. Nothing terrible is going to happen to you.

Helpful thoughts are magical! They can actually stop that awful sick feeling in your stomach from happening. Mindfulness is the key - recognising the bad track, then switching tracks to something more uplifting.

But what if the recorded track is right? What if you *are* terrible at spelling tests? Isn't it doing something helpful? No. This track is pushing down your confidence. It's making you feel bad. How is that helpful? If you want to feel good about yourself, you have to only allow helpful thoughts to have power over you.

Nerves and the Solar Plexus

Sometimes you might hear someone say, "My nerves are bad today." Believe it or not, 'nerves' are real. You have nerves stretching to every part of your body. It's how your brain sends and receives messages about how your body feels in its environment. It makes you the coolest walking, talking machine on the planet! There is actually a meeting place where nerves from many parts of your body meet. It's called a ganglion of nerves, the Solar Plexus. It's right in the center of your chest, behind your stomach.

It's sometimes called 'The pit of your stomach' or your 'gut.' When you are fearful, it gets over stimulated and can cause pain or an uncomfortable, tight feeling. But you can stop it. Even if you have already started to feel scared, your helpful thoughts can *make the fear and the pain go away.*

So, how do you control this horrible feeling in your chest?

Focus

When we concentrate on something it's called 'focus'. Your brain pays attention to this.

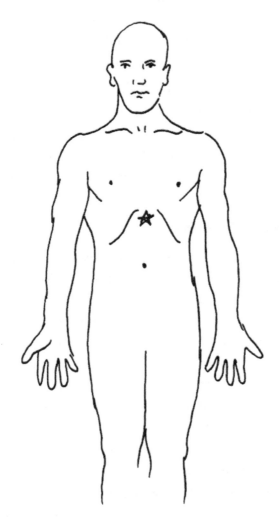

If you are focusing on how terrible you are at spelling, your brain will make your body feel terrible. If you are focusing on how that particular student always teases you and how you get a pain in your stomach, your brain will create the pain in your stomach. But if you are focusing on doing the best you can, relaxing your breathing and the muscles in your body... Aaaaaah! Your brain will obey and make your body relaxed.

Steps you can take

Step 1. Control your breathing.

One of the first things adrenaline does is speed up your heart rate and your breathing. Your mind is so powerful it can actually send a different command to your heart and lungs. YOU can slow them down, just by thinking it! Yes, that's absolutely true. You are in control. Your body obeys your brain and your brain obeys the thoughts and beliefs in your mind.

Step 2. Banish the unhelpful thoughts.

On its own, a thought has no power. Unhelpful thoughts such as: "I can't do this! I feel sick!" *are just thoughts.* They pop in to your mind and they can be sent back out again. You do not have to believe these thoughts. Thoughts become powerful when we believe them. If an unhelpful thought pops in you can tell it to go away by thinking about something else. Distract it!

You could choose to think about something completely different, such as what you're having for dinner tonight, or what you'd like to do when you get home, or imagining yourself playing football for Australia, or winning a dance contest. There are endless possibilities!

Step 3. Relax your body.

If you feel sick in the stomach, you can tell your stomach that its ok, there is no danger, there is nothing wrong, the pain is just a thought, that it can relax now. Place your hands over this spot. Take three or four deep breaths, allowing your stomach to rise and fall with each breath.

Let's try it now!

1. Close your eyes.
2. Let your hands and legs go floppy.
3. Open your jaw slightly (mouth closed) and let your tongue just lie on the bottom of your mouth.
4. Focus upon your breathing. In and out 4 times, nice and deep, but *slowly*. Count to 3, breathing in through your nose and count to 4, breathing out through your mouth.

Now, do you feel relaxed? And guess what? You can do this any time and no one will even know you're doing it.

Foot massage

If you can talk someone into it, get them to give you a foot massage. Many people believe you can make tension in the solar plexus go away by having a foot massage, especially under the ball of your foot (just up from the middle).

Heart packs

Some people also believe that an enormous amount of strength can come from your heart, a feeling of confidence. One way to focus on the feelings in your heart in a positive way, is to use a 'heart pack'. It's just a small wheat bag, heated in the microwave until it's a pleasantly warm and soothing temperature. Not too hot! Then, lie down somewhere comfy and place it on your chest in this area. Relax for as long as you need to, letting the warmth soothe you. Breathe deep. Let a feeling of relaxation drift into your body. It's such a simple thing to do, but it can help a lot. Play some soothing music while you lie there. If you don't have a heart pack, lay your hand over your heart and allow the warmth of your hand to go right through your chest. Remember to breathe deep.

Now, some helpful thoughts to try:

- I can do this!
- I will do my absolute best and not be afraid.
- This isn't scary. That's just a thought.
- This pain in my chest is just because of an unhelpful thought. I can make it go away.
- I'm not perfect. Nobody is.
- Calm down. You can do it!
- Breathe...... Relax your tongue.
- I'm going to think about something nice instead.
- I'll feel better in a minute. I just have to focus on relaxing.
- I'm ok. Nothing is wrong. It's just a thought.
- It will get better soon. I just have to focus on something else.

* Remember – bad thoughts lead to bad feelings. So focus upon positive, happy thoughts for happy, relaxed feelings.

- Dimensions for Heart Pack -

Cut fabric 12cm wide x 24cm long.

Fold in half and sew, leaving a little opening on one side to pour in wheat grains.

Fill to 80% then sew up hole.

Heat for 25-30secs only in the microwave. And then, enjoy!

Chapter Four

Beware the 12 Annoying Monsters

Who's in control?

Because all the sensations in your body are REAL - the tingly legs and arms, the tight feeling in the chest and the hot, sweaty hands & face you *believe that something is really terribly wrong!* Your stomach hurts, there's pain in your chest or a headache. Something is damaged, isn't it?

Nope. It all started with a thought. And thoughts are something you can control. The thoughts that make you panic are like annoying monsters. They start small and grow rapidly. And they all need one thing – to feed on your fears. Each one has a different message. We all hear these monsters, telling us unhelpful stuff in our heads. Some of us have heard almost all of them. See if any of these monsters have been inside your head lately -

Monster #1 Bad Stuff Always Happens to Me!

Figure 1 Monster #1 Bad Stuff Always Happens to Me!

Beware this pathetic monster! He will tell you that bad things only happen to YOU. You are a loser, a magnet for trouble, a hopeless case of bad luck over and over.

But, like all the monsters, he takes a little bit of truth and mixes in a big dollop of fake. The result? You feel sorry for yourself. Feeling sorry for yourself might seem perfectly fair. After all, you're having a crap day and that happens to you a lot. Because you're a hopeless loser. Right? WRONG!

Here's the truth. Your life, like everyone else's, will have good days *and* bad days. It's normal. Everyone experiences it. It's actually ok to have a bad day occasionally. But *how you handle those bad days* will determine how quickly you start to feel better again.

If you start to think thoughts such as:

"Bad things always happen to me!"

It's going to take much longer to feel good again. When you get stuck in these thoughts, thinking that only bad things happen to you, it's a 'self-pity' habit and it can be hard to break. Don't give in to self pity! Don't think like a victim. Good things and not-so-good things happen to *everyone*, not just you.

Monster # 2 – I'm all alone and no one loves me

Figure 2 Monster #2 I'm All Alone and No One Loves Me

This monster taps into your very first memories as a baby. You wanted to be picked up and cuddled, fed, stroked and tickled. A part of you will always be this little baby. And Monster #2 knows this. Sometimes you worry that no one likes you or you might feel afraid to be left alone. It's like a dark, cold room with no windows or doors. But it isn't real. It's just anxiety making you feel this way. The people who love you and care for you are not going to abandon you. Focus on your breathing and tell yourself a helpful thought, such as:

"I know my family loves me.

I'm just feeling a bit anxious right now."

The feeling of loneliness often happens when you feel disconnected from other people. The best thing you can do is *start talking to people*, break out of the loneliness by taking a step towards others. Begin a new hobby or interest. And this doesn't mean finding new friends on the internet, it means REAL people, in person. You can't get hugs from an online chat. Turn off the computer. Talk to someone real. No one will know how you feel if you don't say anything. No one knows you're looking for a new interest if you don't ask. Meeting new people can seem a bit scary, but if you have a backup plan you will feel safe. You *can* do it. It all starts with a helpful thought. Like this:

"I'm going to go to that birthday party and stay for a little while, talk to some people and see how it goes. If I want to, I can leave early, but if it works out, I'll stay".

Another helpful way to control this all alone feeling is to focus on other people, not yourself. Ask questions. Get people talking about themselves. Everyone loves to talk about their own stuff and they love it when someone shows an interest. They feel accepted. So, instead of thinking about how unaccepted you feel, work on showing others that you accept them. See the difference? People will think 'wow, that guy/girl is really nice!' So how do you do this? You start with noticing things. If they have a really cool phone, give them a compliment, such as 'Hey, I like your phone.' And then ask how long they've had it. Then you might ask, 'If you could have any cover you want, what would it be?' If they have a cool bike, or ipod, whatever. The same applies. Begin with noticing what is important to them. Give a compliment to show that you've noticed. Then ask questions to get them talking. You can do it! Don't let this monster control you. You are not alone if you don't want to be.

Monster # 3 - Change is always bad

Figure 3 Monster #3 Change is Always Bad

This monster tells you that it's so comfortable where you are. So nice and safe. Why would you want to change anything? But he keeps you trapped there while you long for something more. He tells you that change is always painful and that you should avoid it.

But change isn't always bad. Change is often the opposite – excellent! It means you are growing, moving ahead, getting wiser, becoming more independent. Change is a normal part of everyone's life. In some ways, change is like a little test you have to pass. You push through your fears, keep calm, and when you get to the other side you feel SO GOOD! You feel stronger.

Sometimes the new things which happen are much better than the old ways you were used to! But you will never know if you don't try. Fear of change can make you panic. But don't give in to it. You can still do things, even if you feel afraid, because feeling afraid doesn't mean you *can't* do it, it just means it's uncomfortable *while* you're doing it.

Did you get that?

You can actually still do stuff, even when you're scared as hell. Be scared…. And do it anyway! If you wait for the confidence to do things, you will probably never do it. Why? Because confidence doesn't come *before* you do something. It comes *because* you do something. Afterwards. Just push through. And when you turn around to see where you've come, you'll feel proud of yourself.

Changes demand that we react and cope with them. You might need some help with that. It's important to talk about your fear of change to someone you trust. Tell them it's freaking you out a bit. Don't be afraid of change – it is usually a good thing, and it's a normal part of your life as you grow.

Monster # 4 – I'm starting to panic!

Figure 4 Monster #4 I'm Starting To Panic!

This monster doesn't negotiate, he just takes over, suddenly, like a crazed military commander, driving a tank over you. And it happens so quickly you don't have time to stop it. Your breathing is too fast, your hands are tingly and there's a pain in your chest already. Monster #4 is in control!

But no, he's not in control, it just feels like it. Accept that it's happening. You started to panic, you're not sure why yet. Just breathe slowly and wait. The adrenaline will eventually stop pumping around your body and everything will return to normal. Tell yourself,

"This feeling is going to subside in a minute. Breathe slowly…"

Watch that your thoughts aren't keeping it going! This monster loves that. He will tell you that this horrible feeling is going to go on and on, that there's nothing you can do to stop it. But, the feeling of panic will slowly go away. It always does. Your body *wants* to return to normal as soon as possible. Give it some time. Tell the panic monster to go away while you breathe…

Monster # 5 – Scared of Feeling Scared

Figure 5 Monster #5 Scared of Feeling Scared

This monster might look quite cute, but he will drive you crazy! He is SO SCARED of being scared and if you believe him, you'll be a quivering wreck. He keeps telling you that being afraid is absolutely terrifying and that you just cannot cope when that happens!

That you MUST avoid being afraid because it's the worst thing in the entire universe! That it's so bad, you'll die! Let's face it. He's a little bit right.

Being frightened is a hideous feeling. Your body reacts with sensations that are so real, you *believe* there is something real to be afraid of and you end up *dreading* that fear. You become afraid of being afraid. You might think:

Oh no! I'm getting that fear feeling again!

I'm going to feel so horrible! Argh!

Hey, the weird thing is that being scared of feeling scared keeps you in a constant state of terror anyway. So how has he helped you?

Remember, fear is a natural thing your mind does to keep you safe. When your fear makes your body react, it is doing its job. It's not a bad thing. It's natural. If there is no real danger, the feeling will pass and you will feel better again. The trick is to relax as much as you can and find something else to think about. This is called **distraction.**

Being afraid of being afraid will keep you prisoner and stop you doing the things you love. Take control! Get busy. Don't let the fear control you. It's just a thought, remember? If it continues and becomes a serious problem, you might need your parents to take you to a doctor to discuss what's happening.

Monster #6 – It's all my fault

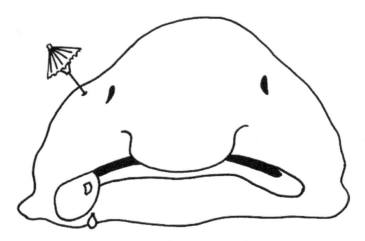

Figure 6 Monster # 6 It's All My Fault

Oh, this monster is pathetic!. He's the twin brother to Monster #1'Bad things always happen to me.' He feels sorry for himself *all the time* and it can get pretty annoying to hear him whining. Unless, of course, you believe him.

People who worry a lot can sometimes think that someone has to be blamed when things go wrong. They blame others, they blame God or they blame themselves. The truth is, it's not that black and white. Sometimes *no one is to blame.* That's right! No one. Sometimes what happens is just an accident. Sometimes you must take responsibility. So, how to tell the difference?

Sometimes we try to keep others happy by taking the blame. We don't want Mum or Dad to get upset. We don't want our friend to get into trouble. We don't want the teacher to be mad at the whole class. So we say 'I did it." Or "It was my fault." When it really wasn't.

While it is very brave and noble of us to stick up for our friends, or to spare our parents the upset, in the end it will make us feel quite useless. Things which are under your direct control, which you are expected to take care of, well, they tend to be the things for which you are responsible. Like feeding the cat, getting your school bag ready the night before or keeping your bedroom tidy.

But what if something freaky happens and it all goes terribly wrong, despite your best efforts? Then it's not your fault. Things just happen sometimes. You are not always to blame. It can't possibly be your fault all the time! Don't listen to this lazy, whining monster. Because he just wants you to feel guilty. For everything. Be brave, when you really have stuffed up. Be honest about it. Take responsibility. Ask for help to do this. You could say, "I'm really sorry. I didn't mean for this to happen. I was a bit careless. I'll do better next time. Will you forgive me?" No one can reject you for that.

And if it's not your fault and you just don't want your Mum or Dad to get angry, then tell them so. "I didn't do it, I just don't want you to get angry. It makes me feel sad and frightened."

When this monster whispers in your head:

It's all your fault and nobody loves you.

It's all your fault. You're a hopeless loser.

It's all your fault. You can never do anything right.

When you hear him say this, tell yourself –

No. It's not my fault. I won't listen to you.

You just want to make me feel miserable. Go away!

45

Monster #7 – Everything must be Perfect

Figure 7 Monster #7 Everything Must Be Perfect!

There is no such thing as perfect! This monster is telling you a big, fat, juicy lie.

You can get yourself tied up in mental knots trying to do things perfectly. And he will always tell you the same message:

That's not good enough. You're useless!

Or worse,

Everything must be perfect or *I won't feel safe.*

And that's the worst LIE of all. He'd love you to think that everything MUST be perfect. Unfortunately, if you listen to him, you won't even bother trying sometimes.

His message is clear –

'If you can't do it perfectly first go, don't even bother trying,

because people will laugh at you for making a mistake.'

Don't listen to him! He's wrong. He doesn't want you to know that everyone makes mistakes and that *that's* how we learn. Whether you're the Prime Minister, a teacher, police officer, scientist, dancer, singer or astronaut, the same is true – we all learn from making mistakes. And that's ok. But if you try to do things absolutely perfectly you will eventually fail at that. And then this monster will tell you another message:

What are your parents going to say?
They'll be so mad at you for this!

Perfection is a slippery slope to Doom Town, my friend. You could spend your whole life trying and trying and still feel not good enough. There is no such thing as perfect.

So what's the answer?

What matters is that you give it a try. Your best try. And if that doesn't work, you will have learned something important for next time. Do your best. That's all you CAN actually do! And others will just have to live with it. Most of the time others aren't that worried about the things we're so obsessed with anyway! They might say:

"It's ok, Honey. That's fine."

And they mean it! It IS fine. Just as it is. If your bedroom is neat and tidy, that's fine. Ok? It doesn't have to be dust mite free and hyper-allergenically clean. If you only got 70% on an exam instead of 89%, forgive yourself for being human. There are many different ways to get to your goals. And being perfect isn't one of them. Do your best. Try your absolute hardest. And accept the outcome. Let go of the need to be perfect or it will control you and make you so unhappy. Be the boss of this monster.

Monster # 8 – I'll never get to sleep!

Figure 8 Monster #8 I'll Never Get To Sleep

This monster actually works quite hard! And he's very sneaky. He gets busy long before you even go to bed. While you're eating dinner he whispers in your ear that you're going to lie awake all night and feel lousy tomorrow and not be able to concentrate on anything. Probably get in trouble for sleeping in class! But don't listen to him. He's not in charge of you.

Sleeping is all about relaxing your mind and your body. And if you can't sleep, don't thrash around in the bedclothes. Read for a while, or get up and do something until you feel sleepy again. Have a drink of warm milk.

The worst thing you can do is to believe his biggest lie of all – that disaster will happen if you don't get any sleep. So what if you don't sleep tonight? You can catch up later. Eventually your body will force you to sleep. The world is not going to end just because you're a bit tired. Sure, your body and your mind need sleep and it's wise to get the hours you need. Most kids need around 10 hours a night. So count back from the time you get up and figure out when you need to go to bed.

Night time routines are very helpful for getting to sleep.

- Begin half an hour before you actually need to be in bed, ready to turn out the light.

- Make sure you've done everything you need to do for tomorrow, so you don't lie there, worrying you forgot something. Perhaps a list of what you should pack in your school bag. Also, that your homework is completed and packed in your bag.

- Brush your teeth, shower, etc.

- Settle into bed and read a book, or do some drawing on a sketch book, or write in your journal.

- Don't use anything with a screen, like a laptop or Gameboy or Nintendo. Bright screens will stimulate you, rather than switch off your brain.

- A cool night light might help. Perhaps one that puts stars on your ceiling.

- Play some soothing music in headphones.

- Set your alarm to go off at the same time each day.

- Practice relaxing every part of your body, beginning with your toes and right up to your head.

Once you've turned off the light, don't worry too much if you can't drift off instantly. Before you realize it, you'll be snoozing. And if you hear the monster whispering in your ear, ignore him! Say,

I'm fine. I'll lie here and think of something else. And if I can't sleep

I'll read for a while. If it takes a while to fall asleep, then that's OK.

Monster # 9 – DO IT NOW!

Figure 9 Monster #9 You Have To Do It Now!

This monster shouts. He is demanding and rude, insisting that you do things right now, or you'll get into serious trouble. He tries to convince you that you must think about these things *all the time*. They're too important to just forget about. Because if you forget, disaster happens. Right?

No. There *are* important things you need to remember or do, but there are also things which *seem* important, but aren't. So, how to tell the difference? How do you tame this monster?

- Write down, on paper, the important things you feel you need to remember or do.

- Look at them. Which ones have to be done right now? Put a star next them.

- Which ones can you leave for a while? Put nothing next to them.

- So, now look at the ones with stars. Pick one. Do it. Cross it off the list. Pick another, (not necessarily today). Do it. Cross it off the list. And so on.

What's interesting is that you will find some of things weren't really urgent at all.

Breathe deeply for a few moments and think.

Patience..... I need to be patient about this and think clearly.

Solutions will present themselves into your mind when you create some space in it that isn't completely gobbled up by anxiety. Ask yourself,

Is this really important right now, or can it actually wait?

And then tell the DO IT NOW monster to buzz off!

Monster # 10 – It's a CATASTROPHE!

Figure 10 Monster #10 It's a Catastrophe!

It doesn't take much to set the catastrophe monster off. He's like a giant spring, ready to... BOING! He loses the plot at the slightest thing, shrieking in your ear. To him, *everything* is *always* a disaster. He doesn't wait to see if things are actually that bad, he explodes inside your head in a frantic voice that it's ALL YOUR FAULT and you're going to get into *terrible trouble*!

Your life is worthless and everyone will *hate* you. And *Just look at what you did! The whole world is going to know!* What's worse, when these so-called disasters happen, he tells you to lie about it, blame someone else, because if they find out it was you, your life will be over. No one could possibly forgive you. And all because you spilled orange juice on the carpet at your friend's house.

But he is a liar, just like the others. He twists the truth until it becomes scary. Yes, perhaps your friend's mum might get a little upset that you spilt orange juice on her lovely white carpet, but if you say, sincerely, that you are sorry and that it was an accident and that you'll be more careful next time, and give her an honest look, how can she be mad at you?

When you think about it, he might look quite cute, but his message is pretty scary. How will you ever feel good about your life if you listen to him? Sure, there will be times when you make a mistake. Big deal! Everyone does. It's not a catastrophe. The ground didn't open up and swallow your friends and family. Be honest about your mistakes. Own up. Be prepared to repay or fix any damage you caused. People will forgive you.

There will be times when you really do think the worst is about to happen. Do me a favour? Take a few deep breaths and wait. Just wait and see, before you run around like a headless chicken. Most times, it's never as bad as you think. Give yourself a moment to see what happens. Perhaps talk to someone about your fears that it's an utter disaster.

Monster # 11 – I have to control everything

Figure 11 Monster #11 I Have To Control Everything

This monster has a terrible appetite. He tells you that YOU HAVE TO BE IN CONTROL of everything, that it won't be right, won't be done properly, unless you do it, because *you are the only person who can do it right*.

He insists that everyone has to do what you want, so that you feel safe. And he jumps up and down, shouting, when things don't go as he expects.

In one sense, he's right. It would be great if everything went exactly how we wanted. There'd be no need to worry about anything at all! Everything would go smoothly and work properly. Every time. Sometimes you might feel as if life is not fair. You always seem to be in the wrong or failing at something. That's when you might start to think that if you controlled everything, it *couldn't* go wrong and you wouldn't have to be upset. So, you begin by controlling those around you – your family. If only Mum and Dad would fit into your system, do what *you* think is best, everything would be fine! And kids at school should behave the way *you* think is right. It would make you feel so much safer, wouldn't it, if things were more predictable?

But what happens when you try to control others? It's a disaster. People get upset when you insist on things done your way. They don't like it. And what about the things you can't control, like a train arriving on time? Or school finishing late because of special assembly? Or the weather turning bad just when you've decided to go outside?

At the bottom of this monster's anxiety is the notion that things must be how you need them to be or you will feel bad, or things will go horribly wrong and that only you can see this. So you try to control things, make them fit, make everything safe.

But is that real life? NO. This monster knows this already. He is trying to convince you that you are not safe unless you know what's going to happen.

So what is the truth?

The truth is, you are not the only person in this universe. You have to live and work and mix with others who also have their own wants and needs. And some of them want things done differently to you. And that is perfectly ok. Just as with the other monsters, you have a choice. You don't actually have to listen to him. His ideas are crap anyway. Who could possibly control everything? It's ridiculous. And what's more, it wouldn't make you feel any safer. There would always be something else he wanted to control. The need to control is this monster's huge appetite. It infects you and won't let go, as long as you keep feeding it.

Wouldn't it feel better if you could allow things to happen and still feel ok about it? Relaxed even! Let others have control sometimes? There's nothing you can do about the train being late, or the assembly dragging on and on. You will only feel worse if you keep allowing this monster to upset you with his lies. Instead, try your relaxation techniques. Takes some nice, big breaths, push the air out of your lungs and say to yourself,

"It's actually ok. I'm perfectly all right.

Nothing bad is going to happen to me."

It's also a good idea to have a Plan B ready.

"If I'm late home, I'll just explain what happened."

I want to add that some children live with family difficulties. There may be conflict at home, (fights) or illness in the family. In these situations it's hard to cope and children have the least amount of power to change anything. If this is your situation and you feel anxious about it, the best thing to do is talk to someone you trust, an adult, who will be able to help you. You might not be able to control what's happening, but you *can* reach out for help.

Monster # 12 – The whole world is a horrible mess!

Figure 12 Monster #12 The Whole World is a Mess!

This monster loves watching the news. There's so much death and suffering in the world and he wants to see it all. And remind you of it later, when you're trying to sleep. He enjoys making you feel scared, unsafe.

If you only ever watched the news, nothing else, you might begin to think the world was indeed a mess. Bad things seem to happen all the time. There's cruelty to animals, cruelty and violence to people, horrific accidents, natural disasters etc. People seem to behave so selfishly to others. But the news isn't real life, just a small part of it, that the news station *chooses to tell you about.* Why? Because bad news sells. All those companies that advertise during the news make heaps of money while everyone waits to see just how bad that cyclone was, how many people died, who got shot, which animals are becoming extinct.

But you don't have to watch. You don't have to accept this version of life on our planet. Life isn't all bad, like TV says. There are many good, kind and helpful people in the world. There are good luck stories and stories of kindness and bravery everywhere. It's also a beautiful place with many natural wonders to see and experience, many different cultures and languages to explore. Many amazing, scientific facts to learn.

That's not to say that if something awful *does* happen to you or your family that you can just forget it. If someone you love dies or is hurt you are dealing with an extraordinary situation, a great deal of emotional turmoil. And you will need help to cope with it. Being alone with your feelings of loss or extreme worry is horrible. That's when others people can help. It's very important that you tell someone how you are feeling, so that you can be reassured that it's normal to feel anxious or sad in this situation.

To know that others may also be feeling the same way is very comforting. But in everyday life, when you find yourself focusing on all the bad stuff that happens, it's time to turn off the TV and do something else. Play a game with your family, read a funny book, watch your favourite movie, get outside and play, ride your bike, go for a walk with a friend, bake a cake with Mum, play with Dad, talk to your friends. The ideas are endless! But they are all positive ideas which get your mind off that depressing track of thought.

Chapter Five

Know and Understand Yourself

Types of People

Everyone is different. Unique. You've heard that before, right? But what is also true is that we are similar to lots of people too. There are *types of personalities*. One of them will fit you quite well. You will find that you are not alone with some of your quirky habits!

Self-Knowledge

Self-knowledge means understanding yourself. You get to understand why you react the way you do. You realize which past events or people have influenced your feelings about yourself. And you learn to accept the characteristics you were born with. Getting to know yourself means facing who you really are, that person you see in the mirror when you are alone. If you don't really like yourself, facing who you are can be painful. But it's only the first step. The goal is becoming a confident, likeable person who attracts friends, isn't afraid of trying new things, who can pick themselves up when they fail. Wouldn't that be absolutely awesome?

Be proud of your strengths

Everyone has personal strengths, attributes which others admire. You might be talented at Art or making things, you might be musical, you might be excellent at helping people, you might be a natural fixer of machines or you might be fantastic at Maths and Science. There is at least one thing you are good at and this you can be very proud of! No one can take it away from you. Appreciating your particular strengths is part of getting to know yourself.

Be brave about your challenges

Everyone also has challenges. These are things you are not so good at. You might struggle with spelling, you might be a bit clumsy or not great at sport, you might blurt things out before you think, you might struggle with rules or not cope well without them. Everyone has at least one challenge. It's part of their personality. No one has only strengths and no challenges. Accepting your particular challenges, unique to you, is part of getting to know yourself.

Natural tendencies and Resilience

Understanding your natural tendencies gives you confidence. You know how you think, what holds you back, what makes you feel strong. Accepting your natural tendencies means taking responsibility for your own thoughts and thus, your actions. It sounds complicated, but it's not. Imagine being fearless! Imagine coping perfectly well with the things that scare you, anger you or tire you out, not letting them stop you from doing anything. Imagine being able to help yourself out of sticky situations. Being able to calm yourself. This is what's called *resilience.* Resilience means you don't always need someone to hold your hand. You can do things yourself, even when they go a bit wrong or not as you expected.

You can learn how to *work with* your natural tendencies, rather than fighting against them or being ashamed of them. You can still achieve your goals, be likeable, be successful, no matter what your fears, (those 12 annoying monsters), try to tell you.

Chapter Six

9 Beliefs that will drive you crazy

Crooked Thinking

A very clever doctor called Albert Ellis came up with the idea of crooked thinking. That is, thoughts which make you unhappy. These beliefs can be quite dangerous, if you let them control your mind. He called them 'Irrational', which means unreasonable, absurd. See if any of them are familiar to you. Here they are:

1. I *must* do well at all times.

2. I am a bad or worthless person when I act in a weak or stupid manner. I *must* be approved or accepted by people I find important.

3. I am a *bad, unlovable* person if I get rejected.

4. People *must* treat me fairly and give me what I need.

5. People who act immorally are undeserving, rotten people. People *must* live up to my expectations or it is terrible.

6. My life *must* have few major hassles or troubles. I *cannot* stand really bad things or difficult people. It is awful or horrible when important things don't turn out the way I want them to.

7. I *can't stand* it when life is really unfair.

8. I *need* to be loved by someone who matters to me a lot.

9. I *need* immediate gratification and always feel awful when I don't get it.

So, did you understand what they mean? Let's take a look at each one and hopefully we can clear up anything you're not sure about.

1. **I *must* do well at all times.**

The problem with this belief –

This statement comes with responsibility that is impossible! No one can do well every single time. And when you tell yourself you MUST, you put enormous pressure upon yourself to perform. This can develop into *Performance Anxiety* - a horrid fear that stops you even attempting things. Aim to do well, putting in your best effort, but no one can do more than their best. Ok?

2. **I am a bad or worthless person when I act in a weak or stupid manner. I *must* be approved or accepted by people I find important**

The problem with this belief –

No wonder this sort of thinking can send you mad! Everyone does silly things at times. There are also times when you don't feel brave enough or confident enough to do things. It's just your brain's way of keeping you safe. For example, if all the other kids want to jump off a huge rock and you feel too scared. That is your right, to protect yourself. It doesn't mean you are a bad person or have no worth.

Being accepted is very important to all of us. As humans we feel safer when we have others around us, parents who care for us and teachers who listen and are kind. But there will be times when you are a bit annoying to other people.

There will be times when your behaviour is a tiny bit selfish. You can't expect everyone to approve of that! People can still love you and accept you, even if they don't like your behaviour at the time.

3. **I am a *bad, unlovable* person if I get rejected.** (If people don't want me to play with them, there is something wrong with me).

The problem with this belief –

There are types of people that we naturally like and want to spend time with and there are people we would prefer to avoid because they are not really our type of person. They don't like the same things or they're too loud or too quiet for us. It doesn't mean they are a bad person, does it? They are just more suited to different friends who like that kind of stuff. Eventually they find the right friends who fit them. The same is true of you.

There might be times when you feel rejected, when others don't want to include you. It doesn't mean you are a bad or unlovable person. And there are lots of reasons why bullies pick on people too. Bullies have big problems of their own that they are struggling with. That's why they pick on others, to make themselves feel better. If a bully picks on you, it's not YOU who has the problem, it's the bully.

If you're starting a new class or new school it can take a while to find the group where you fit and feel comfortable. Give it time. Be friendly. Practice asking questions. Be interested in others.

4. People *must* treat me fairly and give me what I need.

The problem with this belief –

Of course you want people to be nice to you and give you what you need. This is natural. A survival instinct.

Just remember, while you want what you need, everyone else wants what they need. And you can't expect to be top of their list. They have themselves to look out for. And so, there will be times when you are not treated fairly. Guaranteed.

People sometimes make selfish choices. They might tell a lie about what happened in the playground or at the school disco. Your sister might convince your parents that you hit her, when it was actually your sister who hit you. This isn't fair!

But it is going to happen from time to time. Why? Because you are not in control of what other people do. You can ask for what you need, but it's up to the other person to give it to you. Freely. Not because you demand it.

But here's the thing – if you spend some time thinking about what others need or would like, you will spend less time demanding your own stuff. And others will be happy to have you around. And likely give you what you need anyway.

5. People who act immorally are undeserving, rotten people. People *must* live up to my expectations or it is terrible.

It would be wonderful if people always did the right thing, wouldn't it? There would be no need for jails or police. We'd feel safe all the time.

The problem with this belief –

Alas, this is not real life. People who break the law are not always horrible people either. I once heard a woman tell how she ended up a drug addict in jail. She was an ordinary lady with a nice house, job, husband and kids. Then her daughter was killed by a car outside her home. The woman could not cope with her daughter's death and became very ill. She was on medications but that wasn't enough. She turned to drugs to feel better. She lost her home, her husband and ended up stealing to get money for more drugs. That's how she ended up in jail. She wasn't a bad person, she just had something terrible change her life completely and wasn't able to handle it. There are also people who make bad choices, not because they are bad, but perhaps because they didn't have the right advice at the time.

You know what's right, but you will probably come across people who make poor choices and do the wrong thing. They might disappoint you by not returning your call or message. They might ignore you, even though you sent them a birthday card. It's not your fault that they don't do the right thing. And again, you have no control over what other people choose to do. This belief will make you a judgmental, unhappy person.

6. **My life *must* have few major hassles or troubles. I *cannot* stand really bad things or difficult people. It is awful or horrible when important things don't turn out the way I want them to.**

When things go wrong it can feel quite distressing. Hassles and troubles – who wants them? And difficult people are a pain!

The problem with this belief –

Part of being an independent person is learning to cope when things don't go as we would like. We learn to 'bounce back' when we're knocked down. It's actually good for our confidence to have to fight through problems, so don't be scared of that. If you tell yourself that your life is horrible when things don't work out the way you thought they would, you will struggle to be happy. And you do have a choice when people are being difficult.

Most of the time you can actually just walk away. If it's a class project, that is more difficult. Learning to listen to others and trying to understand how they think and feel is helpful. Ask for advice on how to handle the situation. Be honest about your feelings. ie: "I feel disappointed that this didn't work out." Or "I don't like working with Toby. He wants things his own way. Can you help me with this?" But be careful not to blame other people for your disappointment.

7. **I *can't stand* it when life is really unfair.**

Do you hate it when life is unfair to others? We often see things on the news which can be quite distressing. An example would be a young girl who gets brain cancer, or loses both her parents in a car crash. Life is truly unfair to her. And there is nothing you can do about it. This is awful!

The problem with this belief –

Good and bad things happen to everyone. There is not always a reason behind it. Nice people who obey the law and love their family sometimes have horrible things happen to them.

Criminals sometimes get lucky. It's just the way life is. Most of the times good people do well and bad people don't. But sometimes random factors come into it and the opposite happens. Life can be unfair at times.

What's important is that you don't constantly go over this crazy belief in your mind, believing it to be true. Try to focus upon the things that go right, rather than the things which go wrong. If you can, offer to help when life has been unfair to someone.

8. I *need* to be loved by someone who matters to me a lot.

There might be a cool, new kid at school. You desperately want to be friends with this person. But they don't seem interested in you. This person matters a lot to you, but you don't seem to matter a lot to them. They choose others to be their friend. Argh!

The problem with this belief –

As babies we are born with the instinct to demand attention, food, drink. Otherwise we would not survive. As we grow we come to understand that we can't always get what we need exactly when we need it.

We have to wait our turn. The same is true of the acceptance that we want from people who matter to us. It's important to remember that we don't always get what we want, even if we wait a long time. Sometimes we're not meant to have it. Sometimes something better is waiting for us. It won't help if you keep telling yourself that this person *has* to accept you and that you desperately need that to happen.

9. I *need* immediate gratification and always feel awful when I don't get it.

Immediate gratification means getting what you want right now! And it might seem a terrible tragedy if it doesn't happen.

The problem with this belief –

As a baby you cried until you got your dummy. Your mother wanted to keep you quiet, so she gave it to you. But as you grow up, you are expected to wait for things, consider others, share. It's not always easy, but you must tell yourself to be patient. Sometimes having a goal and working towards it can create real excitement and pride when you finally achieve it! Like saving up for a new bike. Working hard towards that goal, saving your pocket money, doing odd jobs to earn extra cash, these are all really good for your self-esteem and confidence.

When you ride that new bike you feel amazing because you did it yourself! You will be fine if you don't get exactly what you want exactly when you want it.

Chapter Seven

What you can do if you feel anxious

Talking

If you feel yourself getting anxious, have that little niggling in your stomach, talk to someone - your mum or your dad, or a sister, brother or friend, perhaps a teacher. Telling someone you feel worried is a very important thing to do if you're going to make the feeling go away. Sometimes just telling someone about it helps you to see that it's not that bad after all and that it doesn't have to take over your life. Others can comfort you in a way that you are unable to do yourself. They can tell you what's real and what is just your imagination.

Forgive yourself

Hey, you're not perfect. You will make mistakes, no matter how hard you try not to. It's normal. Everyone does! Forgive yourself for making a mistake and learn how to do it better next time. Mistakes are actually really good at teaching you. It is life's natural way, because you don't always believe your parents. Sometimes you just have to do it yourself and find out in your own way. Your parents made mistakes when they were growing up. That's how they learned. - from making mistakes. When you make a mistake you might feel bad, but the feeling will pass and you will think, 'Gee, I really learned something important from that mistake!' It's a good thing.

Being likeable

It's impossible for everyone to like you. We are all so different. Do you like absolutely everybody? No. There are some people we just don't click with. And there are people who don't click with us. This is fine. You're not perfect, remember? There will be friends who used to be friends. This can hurt, but as we grow older, we change and sometimes have to leave friends behind. This is an opportunity for you to find new and more interesting friends!

People have their own problems

Sometimes people do or say hurtful things to you. You can think -

'Wow, that's really horrible.

Why did that person do that to me?

What's wrong with me?

What did I do to deserve that?'

But these are unhelpful thoughts that lead only to more pain for you. Everyone has their own problems to deal with. They aren't always thinking about you. Some of them might even have a problem with anxiety and be struggling inside to control it. In general, people don't go around thinking up ways to be nasty to other people. Everyone is too busy with their own lives. And they have their own feelings to deal with. Just be yourself. Be nice to everyone you can. And forgive them readily. They might be struggling too.

Be a good friend

One of the most wonderful things about life is friends. They are there for you when you need them and you can be there for them too. A good way to stop some of your unhelpful thoughts is to focus on doing something nice for someone else. It will make you feel great! Don't you love it when friends are thoughtful of you?

Another simple thing you can do is give compliments to people. Find something nice to say about them and you will not only feel good but make them smile too.

Be your own thought coach

You believe 100% of what you say and 5% of what other people say, so it makes sense to give yourself excellent, encouraging advice!

- Instead of, "I can't." Say, "I will."
- Instead of, "Why do only bad things happen to me?' Say. 'Good things and bad things happen to everyone and that's normal."
- Instead of, 'You're such a loser!" Say, "You're pretty darn awesome, you know!"
- Instead of, "Nothing will ever change." Say, "I can make my own changes."
- Instead of ,"I'm so unhappy." Say, "I won't let my past way of thinking make me unhappy anymore!"

The Magic of Sunlight

The sun on your body stimulates it to process vitamin D, which is a mood enhancer. Sunlight, directly through the iris of your eyes, wakes you up properly and gets your body into the correct sleep pattern. So get some sunlight every day! Breakfast in the garden is the easiest way. Just ten minutes a day will make you feel so much brighter and happier. And make it easier to banish those bad thoughts!

The Magic of Exercise

When you exercise, your body produces endorphins. These are natural 'feel good' chemicals. The easiest exercise is walking, so walk to the bus stop, walk to the shops, walk to school or just walk around your neighbourhood with the dog. Get your family to join you for company. It makes it fun! If walking isn't your thing, there's always swimming, cycling, rollerblading, trampolining, jogging, football, soccer, hockey, ice skating etc. Get your friends to join you! Just get out there and do it. You'll feel invigorated and glad to be alive.

The Magic of Good Food

Eating good healthy food makes your body function better and in turn, makes you feel better. Junk food might give you a sugar hit for half an hour, but then your mood falls back down again. Fresh fruit, vegetables, nuts, dairy foods and meat/fish are all part of a healthy diet. Snack on a nuts and seeds mix in between meals for a quick 'pick-me-up'. When you're out at the shops. Ask for a fresh, yummy juice instead of a cola drink. Avoid processed foods like biscuits, cakes, lots of pasta and lollies.

These will make you feel worse. Freshly prepared food is best. Make your own! There are plenty of great recipes for pizza toppings, stews, salads, fruit dishes etc. It's worth the effort, if it makes you feel better. Ask your parents to help you make good, healthy food for school.

The Magic of Chocolate!

The ONLY junk food that has been proven to lift your mood and that isn't *too* unhealthy is good quality dark chocolate. Choose one with natural ingredients and at least 50% cocoa. Just a little bit!

Nighttime Routines

Getting ready for sleep is an important ritual each night. Winding down after a busy or stressful day is the best way to get your body and mind ready for sleep. The human body needs regular sleep to recharge. While you're asleep your body repairs itself. Also, your mind sorts out all the thoughts and events of the day and files them neatly for your memory to access them later. If you don't get to bed early, you interrupt the body's natural rhythm, called the 'circadian rhythm'. The Circadian Rhythm works with the sun. When the sun goes down, your body starts to wind down. When the sun comes up, your body awakens. When we stay up late and sleep-in we are interrupting this very important cycle, which leads to tiredness, stress and foggy brain during the day.

Nighttime tips:

- Turn off the TV or computer at least an hour before bed.
- Chat to your family.
- Have a hot shower or bath to relax your muscles.
- Drink a cup of warm milk, which contains Tryptophan, a natural sleepy chemical found in dairy products.
- Settle in to bed to read a book or magazine using a bedside lamp.
- Then, when you feel drowsy, turn off the lamp and drift away....

Focus on what you want

You might sometimes feel overwhelmed with all the bad stuff that happens to you or even to others. Perhaps the news on TV depresses you. At times you might lie awake in bed worrying about all the nasty things that could happen tomorrow. There are two things to remember here:

1. Good luck and bad luck happens to everyone. Including you. We all manage to get through the bad luck days. You will too! It's a natural part of life that things don't always go as we plan. And that's ok.

2. If you focus on what *could* go wrong, your mind works towards that, as if it is a goal. Use the amazing power of your brain to focus on what you DO WANT instead. This increases the likelihood that it will happen. Your brain will find ways to make your hopes come true if they become your *goals* and you work towards them. Instead of thinking, "Oh, no, that boy/girl I like at school is going to ignore me all day!" Think:

"I'm going to say hello and smile, even if they don't reply."

So, positive self-talk is extremely important if you want to feel happy with your life. Here are some examples of positive self-talk:

1. Hey, I'm actually ok!

2. I like (friend's name) because...

3. I like .... about myself.

4. I'm really good at ....

5. I have excellent ....

6. People compliment me on my ....

Spend more time thinking about the good stuff. Why waste all your energy worrying? It steals minutes, hours, perhaps even days from your life. Focus on what makes you laugh, feel good, feel energized and let that guide your thoughts.

* Positive thoughts for positive outcomes.

Fuzzy Brain

If you are having panic attacks or feeling depressed or angry a lot your brain may find it hard to think. Thoughts are all jumbled. When someone asks you how you are feeling you really can't explain it. School work could be difficult too, as your brain struggles to listen, understand and keep the information in your head. Don't worry. Nothing bad is going wrong in your brain. It isn't going to be like this forever. You're not stupid. Your brain just needs a break from worrying so much! This is why telling someone is SO IMPORTANT. Sharing your problem cuts it in half! You have support and advice to help you learn to handle your fears. A doctor can refer you to a counselor or psychologist who has skills to help you. They see many children with anxiety problems. They know all the tricks to getting it under control. You can trust them. But the first step is to tell your parents/carers or an adult you trust. This is VERY important.

Making others feel comfortable

So many upsets and arguments could be avoided if we think of others' feelings as much as we do our own. You might feel nervous around some people. They make you feel small or fat or ugly or stupid. But a lot of that is in your mind. If you enter a room feeling like a weirdo, you will act like a weirdo and, hey, people will think: "That girl/guy's a weirdo!" It's up to you. Walk into a room as if you are confident, head up, back straight.

When talking with someone, ask them questions about themselves. Be inquisitive. Get them talking about the things they are interested in. Forget about your own stuff. When you are a good listener and show an interest, others think good thoughts about you and like you more. If you waffle on about your own interests and they don't share them, it's boring and a little bit selfish. Make it easier for people to be friends with you by showing you're interested in their thoughts, ideas and opinions. Communication isn't just about saying what you want to say, it's about making others feel comfortable in your presence.

Jigsaws

Jigsaws are good therapy. It's true! They're colourful, interesting pictures we put together. But the unique and wonderful thing about jigsaws is that you *know* all the pieces will fit together neatly. Some people begin by collecting all the edge bits and doing that first. Some like to choose part of the picture to start with and put that together. It doesn't matter which way you do it. You will get there in the end, because all the pieces are included and they all fit together. There's something about piecing together a jigsaw. It's like it helps to piece together things in your mind.

You could also involve the rest of the family by having it spread on the dining room table. A large piece of felt fabric makes it portable. When it's time for dinner, you just roll it up, jigsaw and all, then roll it out again after dinner.

When you finish and stand back to look at the finished jigsaw you feel a sense of achievement and satisfaction.

Chores can be good therapy

I know, it sounds crazy, doesn't it? But you would be surprised at how soothing doing your same old chores can be. Mowing the lawn is a good one. You push the mower up then back, then up then back, making lines and leaving a fresh-smelling, beautiful lawn behind you that you can proudly say is your work of art. You can race yourself to see how quickly (and properly) you can do those dishes. Before two or three songs on a CD finish maybe. Feeding the dog or cat can actually be a nice chore. You stand and watch them, stroke their fur and chat to them. By doing the same chores every day, life takes on a rhythm, which makes you feel calmer. And that's a good thing for an anxious person.

Dramas

Hey, life is full of them. They are going to happen, whether you like it or not. But it's *how we handle them* that counts. Calm thinking will help you cope with dramas. Don't overdramatise it by making it worse in your mind than it is in reality. Think:

"Ok, I can handle this calmly.

What is the first thing I need to do?"

If you don't take control of those anxious thoughts YOU will become the drama, making other people's lives difficult. You'll be known as a 'drama queen'. Just get on with the job, quietly, calmly and try not to focus on all the things you might think will go wrong. Think about how you want it to turn out and work towards that.

* Positive thoughts for positive outcomes.

Keeping a Journal

If it's too difficult for you right now to talk to someone, why not write down your thoughts in a journal? That way your journal becomes your friend, who listens. It can really help. Later on, when you feel ready, you can show your journal to your parents or an adult you trust and then they will understand what you have been going through. And later, when you start to feel better, you can read about how things were back then and realize how far you've come on your journey to taking back control from those annoying monsters!

The Magic of Steps

When you're anxious about something or feel overwhelmed it's hard to think straight. It's hard to come up with all those helpful thoughts when you're drowning in worry! So here's the easiest and most effect strategy –

Do things one at a time.

It's like being at the foot of a pyramid. You look up and the top is so far away you can't even see it clearly. You start to think: "I'll never get there! It's too hard!"

But think only of the first step, the first thing that you can do and do it. Then, take a breath and think of the next step. And so on. Instead of being overwhelmed by the entire journey, you just focus on the next step to take and before you know it, you've gone the whole journey and done what you had to do!

For instance: Let's say you have a big assignment or project to do. You might think:

"Oh no! This is too big! I can't do this!
I'm going to fail and everyone will laugh at me!"

But if you stop and just breathe, in... out.... And think to yourself,

> "Ok, what's the very first thing I need to do?
>
> Ah, yes, collect information from the library."

Then you are on your way.

Letting Go vs Hanging On

Letting go of things isn't easy, but can be done. Sometimes the things you hang to and worry about are not actually worthy of your time. Giving yourself a hard time about past mistakes or something you forgot to do, or why someone has snubbed you or someone you used to care about who no longer talks to you can make you sick with worry. But are these things really worth worrying about? You won't know unless you ask someone, so that you don't have to figure it out all by yourself. Talk to someone you trust about it. Say, "I need to talk to you about something." Wait for them to reply. And begin.

Crying

This might sound strange, but crying is your body's natural way of releasing feelings. These feelings aren't always sad ones. Frustration can build up inside you. Fears can become too big to handle anymore. Crying helps by getting them out, letting your body take care of your mind for a while. Even adults cry at times. Just because they are grown-ups, doesn't mean they feel great all the time. They feel frustrated or sad or depressed or angry too. So let those feelings out. If you have to scream into your pillow, then do it! If you like being cuddled while you cry, ask for a cuddle. The important thing is, you don't always have to know *why* you're crying. When you've let out those trapped feelings it's easier to understand

and recognize what they were, because the pressure is off. People will understand that you just need to have a good cry.

Depression and Choice

When you feel depressed it is usually because you feel there are no options, you don't have choices, you've been forced into this position by things that have happened.

It's just not true!

There are ALWAYS options and choices. You must look for them. You must believe that your life can get better. Your thoughts are the key.

- Ask someone to help you find options.
- Write down some ideas.
- Discuss them.

When you have found some options you will begin to feel lighter.

When you are anxious, you feel like everything is too much. You can't see what you're supposed to do and you feel like just curling up into a tight little ball and giving up. But you can take back some of the power anxiety has stolen from you. By making small decisions. Just tiny little differences. It might be something as small as: "I'm going to have a shower and get dressed." Or it might be "I'm going to call my friend and ask how she/he is." Little decisions give you the confidence to make other little decisions, then slightly bigger decisions. Before you know it, your life has changed and you're happier.

Feeling Bad and Gratefulness

When you feel bad it can be enormous and feel like it will never go away. Like a huge, ugly monster has trapped you in misery. The truth is, there are people who *aren't* suffering like you. And there are people who are experiencing something far, far worse. One of the easiest things you can do to feel better is to write down on paper all things you are grateful for, no matter how small.

They might be things as small as:

"I'm glad I have my cat. She loves me."

"I'm grateful that my parents are there for me."

"I'm glad I live in a nice house and go to a good school."

"I'm lucky to have a nice teacher."

"I'm glad I have one good friend at school."

Feeling grateful lifts your mood and puts healthier thoughts into your mind. There's another way too - Feeling compassionate.

Others are suffering too. Look around you. There could be someone you know going through a really tough time. Look for the signs. Offer support. Even if it's just to say hello to them and smile.

A Hidden Problem

Anxiety is a hidden problem. Because it's in your head, no one knows what you're going through. It's invisible. You look fine, unless you talk to them about it. Some special people know the signs and can see by your face that you're worried, but most people don't have this skill. They won't know something is wrong unless you say something. Sharing your problems with the right person can relieve you of a heavy burden and help you begin to feel better. Writing your thoughts in a journal can also help because you are at least letting your concerns out of your mind.

Helpful Websites

There are some excellent websites that may explain things for you.

Here is one: www.headroom.net.au .

If you are a teenager, I recommend: www.youthbeyondblue. com.

and these ones for your parents: www.kidsmatter.edu.au,www.kidsinmind.org.au

Create the Reality You Want

How you *see* your life will be how it is. Your thoughts become your feelings, your feelings become your attitudes and your attitudes become your actions.

So what you thought was true *becomes true*. Your life is literally what you make it! So make it what it you want, not what you fear. There are lots of ways of achieving your goals. There are always choices and there are people who will help you if you ask.

Live in this moment.

When you're anxious you might tend to worry about what will happen in the future and forget that you're actually living NOW.

This moment, while you're reading this, is important. It's not just filling in time until the next bad thing happens! Get outside and enjoy natural beauty in nature. Shady trees, cool grass under your feet, a waterfall or lake, a picnic or even just lunch on the lawn. Go for a walk in nature with some friends. Take a look at your loved ones. Smile at them.

Ask them how their day has been and really listen to what they say. Do something positive or relaxing for yourself, no matter how small it is. Life is about all the NOW moments. They become memories. What sort of memories do you want?

You Are a Physical Being

From the moment you were born you were touched, cuddled, soothed, fed, kissed and tickled. Your body needs physical touch. As humans we're meant to live in family groups, where it is safe. But life gets awfully busy sometimes and we forget our physical needs. We spend too much time sitting alone watching a screen, or traveling in a car, or sitting at the table or walking to school. We forget about our body. Until something goes wrong.

But you can be kind to your body. Here are some ideas:

1. Ask for hugs! Hugs bring back that feeling of safety you had as a small child. It's such a simple thing to do. Ask your family. Ask your friends. They're free!

2. If your body is very tense, your muscles will be cramped and sore. Have a hot bath, with a cup of bath salts in it or a hot shower. This will relax all the muscles. Soon your mind will relax too.

3. Fire gaze. In ancient times humans sat around fires telling stories and gazing at the flames. There is something very soothing and relaxing about it. If you don't have an open fire at home, ask your parents to light a candle for you, (in a candle holder of course). When you have a bath, light some candles and turn off the light. The gentleness of candlelight will make you feel better and your thoughts will wander as your eyes stare at the flames.

Finally...

So, here are the key points to remember when you start to panic, feel depressed or feel yourself getting worked up.

1. **Breathe**. Counting 1,2,3 in. Counting 1,2,3,4 out. The trick is to *count, not think*. Block out all thoughts by counting in your head.

2. **Reassure yourself**. Pop a helpful thought in your head, such as "I'm ok. This feeling will pass in a moment."

3. **Focus.** Think of something pleasurable, such as a nice place you like to go that's peaceful, or imagine a scene where you are extremely happy and proud of yourself.

4. **Decide.** Make a small decision to do something positive, even if it's just to call a friend.

5. **Reach out.** Talk to someone. There are people who could help you, but you have to reach out to them.

6. **Do something fun!** Do I really have to explain this?

7. **Think of someone else.** Think of something you can do for someone else. Plan what you will do and imagine the happy look on their face.

8. **Be patient with yourself.** This will soon pass. Follow the steps and allow yourself some time to feel better. Tell yourself positive thoughts, like you are your own thought coach and notice the difference it makes to your feelings.

Hello!

I promised to see you at the end of the book and here I am. Did you learn some interesting facts? Did you understand what has been happening to you? Isn't it amazing to know that lots of people feel the same way? I bet you had some giggles at some of those monsters. Perhaps Mum or Dad commented on them too. I hope you have found my tips helpful and that you have already started to change the way you think. You do have a choice, you know! When you recognize one of those annoying monsters is talking inside your head, you can tell him to buzz off and give you some peace! Because he is not going to stop you from doing what you love to do. Remember to talk about it to someone you trust.

Good luck in the future! Stay positive! And if you want to drop me a line you can do so here: dawnmeredith1@gmail.com. I would love to hear from you!

Best wishes,

Dawn x

PS I have one more monster for you! But he's a good guy. His messages are always positive...

Hey! You're pretty awesome, you know!
You can do this! Be brave and try your best.
One step at a time and you'll be fine.
It's ok to ask for help.

Figure 13 Monster #13 Happy Guy!

References and influential books

- Aisbett, B., (2002) *Fixing It. The complete guide to anxiety-free living.* Harper Collins Sydney, Australia

- Biddulph, S., (1997) *Raising Boys* Harper Collins, Great Britain

- Doidge, N., (2007) *The Brain That Changes Itself*, Penguin Books, England.

- Gerhardt, S., (2011) *Why Love Matters – How Affection Shapes a Baby's Brain,*

- Kehoe, J., (2005) *Mind Power Into the 21st Century* Zoetic, Vancouver, Canada

- Klass, P., Costello, E., (2005) *Quirky Kids,* Ballantine Books, (Random House) NY, USA

- Littauer, F., (2003) *Personality Plus* Fleming H. Revell (Baker Book House) Michigan, USA

- McCleod, John (2010) *An Introduction to Counselling,* McGraw Hill Open University Press, New York USA (Ellis' Nine irrational thoughts)

- Pease, A. & Pease, B., (2006) *The Definitive Book of Body Language* Pease International, Sydney Australia

- Rapee, R., Spence, S., Cobham, V., Wignall, A., (2000) *Helping Your Anxious Child* New Harbinger Publications, CA. USA.

- Siegel, D., & Payne Bryson, T., (2011) *The Whole Brain Child* Robinson, UK.

- Winston, R., (2002) *Human Instinct* Bantam Books Great Britain, Sussex, UK.

- Kindlon, D., Thompson, M., (2000) *Raising Cain.* Penguin Books, London, UK.

Made in the USA
Monee, IL
14 October 2022